FRANCIS FRITH'S

SUDBURY, LAVENHAM AND LONG MELFORD

PHOTOGRAPHIC MEMORIES

CLIVE PAINE was born and educated in Bury St Edmunds and apart from his years at university, he has worked there all his life. He is a teacher, lecturer, author and broadcaster on all aspects of local history. He has taught History and Local History for 30 years, 21 of which were as County Advisory Teacher for Archives and Local History in Suffolk. He has been a part-time lecturer in Local History for the Cambridge University Institute of Continuing Education for over 20 years. His publications include 'Hartest: A Village History'; 'The Culford Estate'; 'The History of Eye'; 'The Spoil of Melford Church' (with David Dymond); Francis Frith's 'Bury St Edmunds'; 'The Suffolk Bedside Book'; and Francis Frith's 'Suffolk - A Second Selection', 'Suffolk Villages' and 'Suffolk Living Memories'. He frequently broadcasts on local and national radio, and has appeared with Prince Edward on his 'Crown and Country' series for ITV; he has also been profiled in 'Reader's Digest'. He is a Council member of the Suffolk Institute of Archaeology and History and of the Executive of the Suffolk Local History Council, and a past Chairman of the Education Committee of the British Association for Local History. He is also a Lay Reader at St Mary's in Bury.

FRANCIS FRITH'S
PHOTOGRAPHIC MEMORIES

SUDBURY, LAVENHAM AND LONG MELFORD

PHOTOGRAPHIC MEMORIES

CLIVE PAINE

First published in the United Kingdom in 2005 by
Frith Book Company Ltd

Limited Hardback Edition Published in 2005
ISBN 1-85937-849-8

Paperback Edition 2005
ISBN 1-85937-850-1

British Library Cataloguing in Publication Data

Francis Frith's Sudbury, Lavenham and Long Melford -
Photographic Memories
Clive Paine

Frith Book Company Ltd
Frith's Barn, Teffont,
Salisbury, Wiltshire SP3 5QP
Tel: +44 (0) 1722 716 376
Email: info@francisfrith.co.uk
www.francisfrith.co.uk

Printed and bound in Great Britain

Front Cover: **SUDBURY**, *The Market 1904* 51157t
Frontispiece: **SUDBURY**, *North Street 1895* 35469

*The colour-tinting is for illustrative purposes only, and is not intended
to be historically accurate*

Acknowledgements
My thanks, for sharing their local knowledge, go to Liz Wigmore,
Pam Passmore, Margaret and Ernest Shaw, and my wife Christine,
who also read the proofs. Jane Cummins again brilliantly deciphered
my handwriting to set the text. Any mistakes, however, in word or
fact are of course mine alone.

CONTENTS

FRANCIS FRITH
VICTORIAN PIONEER

FRANCIS FRITH, founder of the world-famous photographic archive, was a complex and multi-talented man. A devout Quaker and a highly successful Victorian businessman, he was philosophical by nature and pioneering in outlook.

By 1855 he had already established a wholesale grocery business in Liverpool, and sold it for the astonishing sum of £200,000, which is the equivalent today of over £15,000,000. Now a very rich man, he was able to indulge his passion for travel. As a child he had pored over travel books written by early explorers, and his fancy and imagination had been stirred by family holidays to the sublime mountain regions of Wales and Scotland. 'What lands of spirit-stirring and enriching scenes and places!' he had written. He was to return to these scenes of grandeur in later years to 'recapture the thousands of vivid and tender memories', but with a different purpose. Now in his thirties, and captivated by the new science of photography, Frith set out on a series of pioneering journeys up the Nile and to the Near East that occupied him from 1856 until 1860.

INTRIGUE AND EXPLORATION

These far-flung journeys were packed with intrigue and adventure. In his life story, written when he was sixty-three, Frith tells of being held captive by bandits, and of fighting 'an awful midnight battle to the very point of surrender with a deadly pack of hungry, wild dogs'. Wearing flowing Arab costume, Frith arrived at Akaba by camel sixty years before Lawrence of Arabia, where he encountered 'desert princes and rival sheikhs, blazing with jewel-hilted swords'.

He was the first photographer to venture beyond the sixth cataract of the Nile. Africa was still the mysterious 'Dark Continent', and Stanley and Livingstone's historic meeting was a decade into the future. The conditions for picture taking confound belief. He laboured for hours in his wicker dark-room in the sweltering heat of the desert, while the volatile chemicals fizzed dangerously in their trays. Back in London he exhibited his photographs and was 'rapturously cheered' by members of the Royal Society. His reputation as a photographer was made overnight.

VENTURE OF A LIFE-TIME

Characteristically, Frith quickly spotted the opportunity to create a new business as a specialist publisher of photographs. He lived in an era of immense and sometimes violent change.

For the poor in the early part of Victoria's reign work was exhausting and the hours long, and people had precious little free time to enjoy themselves. Most had no transport other than a cart or gig at their disposal, and rarely travelled far beyond the boundaries of their own town or village. However, by the 1870s the railways had threaded their way across the country, and Bank Holidays and half-day Saturdays had been made obligatory by Act of Parliament. All of a sudden the working man and his family were able to enjoy days out and see a little more of the world.

With typical business acumen, Francis Frith foresaw that these new tourists would enjoy having souvenirs to commemorate their days out. In 1860 he married Mary Ann Rosling and set out on a new career: his aim was to photograph every city, town and village in Britain. For the next thirty years he travelled the country by train and by pony and trap, producing fine photographs of seaside resorts and beauty spots that were keenly bought by millions of Victorians. These prints were painstakingly pasted into family albums and pored over during the dark nights of winter, rekindling precious memories of summer excursions.

THE RISE OF FRITH & CO

Frith's studio was soon supplying retail shops all over the country. To meet the demand he gathered about him a small team of photographers, and published the work of independent artist-photographers of the calibre of Roger Fenton and Francis Bedford. In order to gain some understanding of the scale of Frith's business one only has to look at the catalogue issued by Frith & Co in 1886: it runs to some 670 pages, listing not only many thousands of views of the British Isles but also many photographs of most European countries, and China, Japan, the USA and Canada - note the sample page shown on page 9 from the hand-written Frith & Co ledgers recording the pictures. By 1890 Frith had created the greatest specialist photographic publishing company in the world, with over 2,000 sales outlets - more than the combined number that Boots and WH Smith have today! The picture on the next page shows the Frith & Co display board at Ingleton in the Yorkshire Dales (left of window). Beautifully constructed with a mahogany frame and gilt inserts, it could display up to a dozen local scenes.

POSTCARD BONANZA

The ever-popular holiday postcard we know today took many years to develop. In 1870 the Post Office issued the first plain cards, with a pre-printed stamp on one face. In 1894 they allowed other publishers' cards to be sent through the mail with an attached adhesive halfpenny stamp. Demand grew rapidly, and in 1895 a new size of postcard was permitted called the court card, but there was little room for illustration. In 1899, a year after Frith's death, a new card measuring 5.5 x 3.5 inches became the standard format, but it was not until 1902 that the divided back came into being, so that the address and message could be on one face and a full-size illustration on the other. Frith & Co were in the vanguard of postcard development: Frith's sons Eustace and Cyril continued their father's monumental task, expanding the number of views offered to the public and recording more and more places in Britain, as the

5						+	
6		St Catherine's College		+			
7		Senate House & Library		+			
8					+		
9		Gerrard Hostel Bridge		+	+		
30		Geological Museum		+	+	+	+
1		Addenbrooke's Hospital			+		
2		St Mary's Church			+		
3		Fitzwilliam Museum, Pitt Press &c			+		
4					+		
5	Buxton, The Crescent					+	
6		The Colonnade				+	
7		Public Gardens				+	
8						+	
9	Haddon Hall, View from the Terrace					+	
40	Millers Dale,					+	

coasts and countryside were opened up to mass travel.

Francis Frith had died in 1898 at his villa in Cannes, his great project still growing. The archive he created continued in business for another seventy years. By 1970 it contained over a third of a million pictures showing 7,000 British towns and villages.

FRANCIS FRITH'S LEGACY

Frith's legacy to us today is of immense significance and value, for the magnificent archive of evocative photographs he created provides a unique record of change in the cities, towns and villages throughout Britain over a century and more. Frith and his fellow studio photographers revisited locations many times down the years to update their views, compiling for us an enthralling and colourful pageant of British life and character.

We are fortunate that Frith was dedicated to recording the minutiae of everyday life. For it is this sheer wealth of visual data, the painstaking chronicle of changes in dress, transport, street layouts, buildings, housing, engineering and landscape that captivates us so much today. His remarkable images offer us a powerful link with the past and with the lives of our ancestors.

THE VALUE OF THE ARCHIVE TODAY

Computers have now made it possible for Frith's many thousands of images to be accessed almost instantly. Frith's images are increasingly used as visual resources, by social historians, by researchers into genealogy and ancestry, by architects and town planners, and by teachers involved in local history projects.

In addition, the archive offers every one of us an opportunity to examine the places where we and our families have lived and worked down the years. Highly successful in Frith's own era, the archive is now, a century and more on, entering a new phase of popularity. Historians consider the Francis Frith Collection to be of prime national importance. It is the only archive of its kind remaining in private ownership. Francis Frith's archive is now housed in an historic timber barn in the beautiful village of Teffont in Wiltshire. Its founder would not recognize the archive office as it is today. In place of the many thousands of dusty boxes containing glass plate negatives and an all-pervading odour of photographic chemicals, there are now ranks of computer screens. He would be amazed to watch his images travelling round the world at unimaginable speeds through internet lines.

The archive's future is both bright and exciting. Francis Frith, with his unshakeable belief in making photographs available to the greatest number of people, would undoubtedly approve of what is being done today with his lifetime's work. His photographs depicting our shared past are now bringing pleasure and enlightenment to millions around the world a century and more after his death.

SUDBURY, LAVENHAM AND LONG MELFORD
AN INTRODUCTION

THE PHOTOGRAPHS in this collection cover the period from the 1890s to the 1960s. All the towns and villages are in the ancient Babergh Hundred of Suffolk and the adjacent villages in Essex. This area in the south-west of Suffolk is famous for its so-called wool villages and churches, including Lavenham, Long Melford, Sudbury, Monks Eleigh and Chelsworth. However, it was not the production of the wool which gave rise to immense wealth in the Middle Ages, but the organised production and export of woollen cloth.

By the early 14th century Babergh was a specialist cloth manufacturing area, with spinners, weavers, shearemen, fullers and dyers. The area mainly produced broadcloths, but narrows or streytes were made at the Waldingfields. The cloth was usually coloured, except for the cloth made in the area west of Long Melford, including Stanstead and Glemsford, which was white. Lavenham cloth was mainly blue, in all its shades, or red. Woad produced the blue dye, and madder, grown at Waldingfield, the red dye. The term 'dyed in the wool' comes from the local practice of dying the yarn before it was woven into cloth. Such was the wealth of the Babergh area that Lavenham in 1397 ranked as the 70th most wealthy town in England; it had risen to 14th by 1524, paying more tax than Gloucester, Lincoln or York.

Sudbury had a market at the time of Domesday in 1086. The freemen of the town were granted rights over 44 acres of land on either side of the River Stour in 1260 by Richard de Clare, Earl of Gloucester and Hereford. The lands called Portmannes Croft and Kingsmarsh, from which several of the photographs were taken, are still in the possession of the freemen. The town obtained borough status from Queen Mary in 1554, and was the earliest borough created in West Suffolk.

With the decline of woollen cloth manufacture before the Civil War, much of the area turned to the carding and combing of wool and the production of yarn for spinning at Norwich or Colchester. In the 18th century, when in its turn this trade declined, new sources of employment were developed. For example, silk weaving began at Sudbury in the late 18th century, where by 1851 there were four factories employing around 850 people. Silk weaving was also established at Long Melford, Glemsford and Cornard. Horsehair weaving was introduced at Long Melford in the 1830s by John Churchyard. A factory had been established at Lavenham by c1853 by Churchyard and his son-in-law William Roper, who later developed mat-making using coconut fibre.

Glemsford is a rare example of the creation of an industrial economy in a rural context. In the 1820s the parish officials, faced with problems of high unemployment and high poor rates, took the initiative: they erected a building and offered it rent free for a year to any manufacturer on condition that the locals were employed. In response, a silk factory from Spitalfields relocated here, which was later to have branches at Sudbury.

Before the Dissolution of 1535-39, Suffolk had a large number of abbeys, priories, friaries and nunneries. This gave rise to the term 'selig Suffolk' (meaning 'holy', not 'silly'). At Sudbury the monks of Westminster Abbey founded a cell at St Bartholomew's, north of the town. The Dominican friars had established a friary before 1247 in the street to which they gave their name. Archbishop Simon of Sudbury founded a college of priests in 1375 adjacent to St Gregory's church. Sudbury also had two medieval hospitals, St John's by Ballingdon Bridge and St Leonard's, for lepers, founded c1372 by John Colneys in Melford Road. At Monks Eleigh the monks of Canterbury were patrons of the living and took precedence over the local church officials. Most villages had social and religious guilds. At Lavenham, the famous Guildhall of Corpus Christi stands in the market place, and

SUDBURY, *The Police Station 1906* 55551

the lesser-known Guildhall of Our Lady is now part of the Swan Hotel. Examples of private charities helping the poor can be seen at Long Melford, where Sir William Cordell founded the Hospital of the Holy Trinity as an almshouse in 1573, and at Brent Eleigh, where almshouses were given in 1731 by Edward Coleman.

In the medieval period every parish had its church, most of which had been recorded in 1086 in the Domesday Book. Many of the churches were rebuilt in the 15th century as a thanksgiving for new-found wealth. Much of this wealth derived from the woollen cloth trade. The magnificent churches at Lavenham and Long Melford were built mainly of stone to reflect their status. Other woollen cloth churches are at Sudbury, Great and Little Waldingfield, Glemsford and Stanstead.

In this collection, churches form the backdrop to nearly half the photographs. The churches are in a commanding position in the community; they are mainly built of the local flint, which was also used in the flushwork decoration of the parapets, buttresses and towers. The few churches that are built of stone, which was brought into Suffolk from Rutland and Northamptonshire, are those with the greatest expenditure lavished upon them. Victorian restorations of the high-church movement resulted in the interior of St Peter's, Sudbury and the exteriors of Foxearth and Middleton.

Suffolk was a county of landed estates. In the late 19th century nearly 60% of the land was contained within estates of over 1,000 acres. Many of these estates were sold between the wars; many of the houses that they served were demolished between 1920 and the 1960s.

Photographs of Wood Hall, Sudbury, Long Melford, Kentwell, and Ballingdon show manor houses – Ballingdon has the distinction of having moved site in 1972.

The medieval and Tudor timber-framed jettied houses in Suffolk towns and villages are as much part of the landscape as the trees from which they were constructed. In the 18th century, many houses were re-fronted in plaster or brick, to give them a more modern appearance. In the late Victorian period, when the Tudor 'Golden Age' was in fashion, old houses which had been plastered over had beams painted onto them. Examples of this can be seen in Stour and Cross Streets in Sudbury, where the paintwork and extra timbers have now been removed. From the 1960s onwards, the trend developed (now mainly halted) of exposing the whole timber framing, revealing far more than was intended by their original builders. The photographs of town and village streets all include timber and re-fronted timber buildings, but none is surpassed by Lavenham, closely followed by Chelsworth, Long Melford, Sudbury and Brent Eleigh.

Brick has been used as a local building material since the 15th century, and very widely in the 18th and 19th centuries. There are excellent examples of brick re-fronting or houses built of brick in Sudbury during the 18th century at Wood Hall, Lloyds Bank, and Gainsborough's House, and in the 19th century at Belle Vue, St Leonard's, the Grammar School, and Mattingley's shop in Friars Street. Examples from the 20th century are the Police Station and the County Cinema. Brick buildings elsewhere include the Tudor mansions of Long Melford and Kentford Hall, and the Holy Trinity

Almshouses, and also the 18th-century brick almshouse at Brent Eleigh and the façades of houses around Melford Green.

There were brick kilns at Little Cornard and Bulmer - Bulmer still produces hand-made bricks and tiles. They provided red and white bricks used all over the Stour valley and beyond. The Stour Navigation was used to transport bricks for the building of the Royal Albert Hall and Kensington Museum.

Suffolk and the Stour valley was the home of two outstanding painters in the 18th century. John Constable (1776-1837) was born at East Bergholt, and Thomas Gainsborough (1727-88) at Sudbury. The photographs include many links with the life and work of Thomas Gainsborough. His parents are buried in St Gregory's churchyard; the house in which he was born in 1727 stands in the street re-named to commemorate him; the Independent Chapel in Friars Street is where he was baptised in May 1727; and the Victorian grammar school replaced the building in which he was educated and where his uncle Humphrey was Headmaster. Friars Street contains Buzzards, the home of his Uncle Thomas, and No 31, the home of his cousin Mary, where his daughters Mary and Margaret were born in 1750 and 1751. The two girls were later painted in 'The Artist's Daughters chasing a Butterfly' in 1756. Robert and Frances Andrews of Auberies, the Mr and Mrs Andrews of one of Gainsborough's most famous paintings (created in 1749), lived in the parish of Bulmer. Finally, there is the statue of 1913 in front of St Peter's Church overlooking the Market Hill.

There are several important literary links with the area covered by the photographs. The Rev John Hopkins, Rector of Great Waldingfield from 1561 to 1570, was the author (with Thomas Sternhold) of the first complete book of metrical psalms, published in 1562, which can claim to be the first national English hymn book. The Rev Samuel Crossman was Rector of All Saints', Sudbury from 1647 to 1662. He was a hymn

SUDBURY, *The Croft and the Roman Catholic Church 1900* 45076

writer, best known for 'Jerusalem on High my song and city is' and for the Good Friday hymn 'My Song is love unknown, my Saviour's love for me'. The Rev William Gurnall was Rector of Lavenham from 1644 to 1679. He wrote a commentary on Ephesians Chapter 6 verses 10-16, which became a standard Puritan text for holy living. This was 'The Christian in Complete Armour, or a Treatise of the Saints' War against the Devil', and it appeared in two instalments in 1655 and 1657. Its 1,064 pages work out at 152 pages of comment for each biblical verse.

Charles Dickens used his visit to Sudbury to report an election as the basis for the Eatanswill of 'The Pickwick Papers' in 1837. Mr Pickwick arrived in the middle of an election campaign. Several of the inns mentioned in the book can be identified today, and the hustings took place outside the Town Hall, near Old Market. The next day Pickwick was guest of honour at a fancy-dress literary breakfast at Mrs Leo Hunter's

house, The Den (which may well be the earlier Belle Vue), where she recited her 'Ode to a Dying Frog'. George Fulcher of Sudbury was a printer, a poet, and the publisher of an annual Memorandum Book, to which the Quaker poet Bernard Barton contributed. Fulcher saw himself as the successor to the poet George Crabbe in his defence of the poor against oppressive authority. In his 'Village Paupers' (1845), he highlighted the harshness of the New Poor Law. The Sudbury Union Workhouse features in several of the photographs along the River Stour.

Change has been rapid since the 1960s in areas such as rural employment, transport, housing and educational and shopping facilities. The impact of London overspill in and around Sudbury, and the desire for a pleasant environment for retirement and second homes, make the 1960s photographs seem distant memories. They record as lost a way of life as those from the 1890s.

GLEMSFORD, *Tye Green c1960* G235005

SUDBURY

SUDBURY, *St Bartholomew's Church 1904*
51166

A Benedictine priory belonging to Westminster Abbey
was established here to the north of Sudbury c1130.
This is the 15th-century chapel with nave and chancel
in one. The building survived the Dissolution of 1536
and the clearance of the site in 1779; since then it was
used as a barn. An annual service was held here until
c1830.

SUDBURY *from the air 1929* AF25896

SUDBURY
Wood Hall 1904 51164

The manor house of Wood Hall was owned by the Jones family in the early 19th century. In the 1901 census it was occupied by the Rev William Courtnell, a retired Congregational minister. On 15 October 1944 a B17 Flying Fortress hit the house, which resulted in the death of 15-year-old Raymond Smith. The house was later demolished, and a branch of Tesco stands in its grounds. In 1999 a plaque was unveiled to commemorate the tragedy.

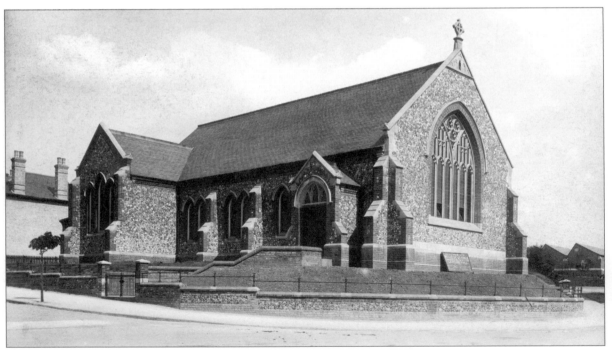

SUDBURY, *The Wesleyan Church 1904* 51165

Situated on the corner of York Road and Girling Street, St John's was designed by Josiah Gunton of London and opened in April 1902. It is built of red brick, Bath stone and flint in a mixture of Gothic styles – there are Early English lancets in the nave and transepts and a Perpendicular west window. This could be a Victorian suburban Anglican church. The minister in 1904 was the Rev William Brown, who lived in York Road.

SUDBURY
York Road, the Wents
1906 55550

This was taken from Queen's Road looking west towards Melford Road in the distance, where we can see Victoria Terrace of 1858 to the right. On the left are one single house and three pairs of 1890s houses, built in white brick with decorative window heads and bands of brick. The open-work garden walls have gone, and several front gardens are now open parking spaces. Beyond to the left is the roof of St John's Wesleyan Church of 1902.

SUDBURY, *North Street 1895* 35469

We are looking north from Old Market. On the right is the White Horse, run by George Rampling; next door is Boggis's the drapers in the 18th-century building with dormer windows; then comes William Alston's 'Second Hand Furniture Warehouse' and the Green Dragon run by Arthur Viall - these last two were replaced in the 1960s. The first-floor bay window just visible beyond is dated 1876 in mosaic, and beside it is the entrance to the North Street Schools. On the left is Angelo Smith's Clockhouse, opened in 1886 and still trading, and, by way of contrast, the Albion Temperance Hotel.

SUDBURY, *The War Memorial 1923* 73609

This is the north end of North Street with the Masonic Lodge off to the left. The war memorial was dedicated in October 1921. It now includes the names of the fallen in both world wars and in Northern Ireland, and also the five civilian victims of a Zeppelin raid in March 1916. The names are now in bronze panels rather than cut into the plinth. The memorial was moved to the green outside St Gregory's in the 1970s. All the buildings on the left were demolished in the 1960s and 1970s.

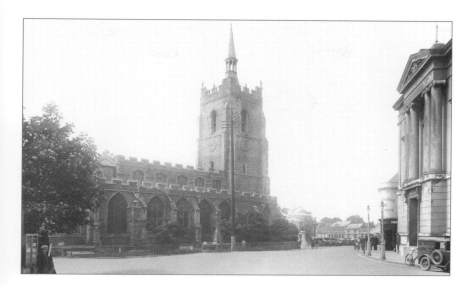

SUDBURY
St Peter's Church 1932
85140

This is taken from Old Market. St Peter's was a chapel-of-ease to St Gregory's, hence it is virtually land-locked without a churchyard. On the right is the Town Hall, with a van from the Radio Supply Company outside. Ahead is the Market Hill with Friars Street in the distance. The buildings include Lloyds Bank, Andrews Stores and the Midland Bank. Off to the left is the corner of Alston's children's wear shop, now rebuilt.

SUDBURY, *The Town Hall 1895* 35481

The Town Hall was built in 1826 on the site of the Exchange Inn, a property belonging to the Borough. Designed by Thomas Ginn of Sudbury, it has three bays with a central pediment supported by four Ionic columns. To the right in Old Market is the general furnishers and ironmonger's of John Simpson, with an advert for Singers and Norwich Union outside. The three-storey building is James Harding the chemist's. In the foreground a girl poses with hands on hips, while a boy laughs at her antics.

21

▼ **SUDBURY,** *St Leonard's Hospital 1900* 35476

The medieval leper hospital of St Leonard's was in Melford Road, where Colneys Close is named after John Colneys, who founded the hospital in 1372. The hospital (for two inmates and a governor) survived the Reformation and continued as an almshouse until 1813. The endowment was used to support the new St Leonard's Hospital, which was established in 1867 in Newton Road.

► **SUDBURY**
The Park c1965
S472066

A Georgian house called Belle Vue was built at the foot of Newton Road in the 1780s. This was demolished in 1871 and replaced by this house, which was built for Edmund Stedman, the Town Clerk
The building became the Borough Offices from c1918 until 1974. This is the south side of the house, which is now the Sudbury Learning Centre.

◄ SUDBURY
*The Police Station
1906* 55551

This was built in 1901 at the junction of Newton Road, King Street and Cornard Road. The police establishment comprised an inspector, a sergeant, and four constables. To the right is Borehamgate House, demolished in 1965 for a shopping precinct. The police station was demolished after the opening of the new station in Acton Road in 1967 - the site is now a wooded traffic island. The Royal Oak run by George Wells for Ind Coope is on the left.

► SUDBURY
The Hospital 1907
58908

St Leonard's Hospital was founded in 1867 for '... the relief and treatment of poor persons suffering from accident or curable diseases'. Visiting hours were from 2-4 on Tuesdays and Fridays and 4-6 on Sundays. Between 1900 and 1907 the left wing was heightened to two storeys. The hospital is still in use today.

▼ **SUDBURY,** *The Cemetery 1900* 35482

The Sudbury and Ballingdon Cemetery was opened in 1859 in Newton Road. The two chapels, Anglican and Nonconformist, are linked by an archway, and stand in the centre of the cemetery. The taller stone in the foreground is for George Grimwood, who died in 1865; he was one of the founders of the Sudbury firm of builders and architects. In 1900 William Ranson was Clerk to the Burial Board, and James Sparrow was the curator who lived in the lodge gate.

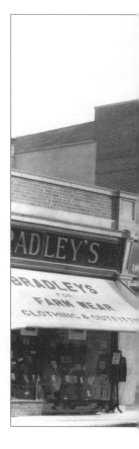

► **SUDBURY**
King Street c1955 S472001

Unlike most photographs of King Street, this view is virtually unchanged. On the right, the Royal Oak, the shop with the arched door and window, and the building nearest the camera, here Dolly's sweet shop, all remain. Just off to the left is Borehamgate Surgery, now the Borehamgate Precinct. The two brick buildings on the left are now Huffer's and Mill House Fabrics. The scene is not so tranquil today, thanks to the traffic.

*King Street and the County
Cinema 1934* 86206

The cinema and the row of shops
were built in the 1930s on the site of
the Rose and Crown Hotel, which
was destroyed by fire in 1922.
The red brick cinema with its
Georgian front was similar in design
to the Local Authority Offices of the
period. The smartly dressed
commissionaire, just visible in the
doorway, welcomed patrons to both
'the pictures' and the restaurant on
the first floor. The cinema was
demolished as part of the post-war
redevelopment, and its replacement
building eventually became part of
Winch & Blatch. The British
Argentine Meat Shop Co (to the left
of the cinema) became Dewhurst's.

▶ **SUDBURY**
Market Hill 1900
45067

The grandeur of both
St Peter's and Market Hill
are shown to best
advantage in the days
before car parking. On
the right, market stalls
are being set up, and
ahead children gather in
expectation of market
day. On the left a
policeman pauses under
the awning of Wright's
the family grocers, later
to become E W King's.
Ahead in Old Market is
the now demolished
Bon Marche.

SUDBURY, *Market Hill 1900* 45068

In the foreground horse-drawn reaping machines are offered for sale in the market. The nearest shop is Robert Joy's, general draper and silk mercer, who also had a shop on the opposite side of the market. In the middle is Bruno, baker and confectioner, with a large Regency window in the first floor. To the left is Arthur Brook's glass and china shop.

SUDBURY, *The Market 1904* 51156

Sudbury had a corn and cattle market on Thursdays and a general market on Saturdays. In the foreground, a harrow and reaping machines are for sale; a crowd on the left is captivated by a sales pitch; outside the church, a Punch and Judy show is under way: while to the right a horse and cart passes Frederick Bowles's milliner and draper's shop and the International Tea Company, adjacent to Lloyds Bank.

SUDBURY
The Market 1904 51156A

Outside St Peter's Church tower a crowd concentrates on the Punch and Judy show. There is a group of carriages parked to the left. In the foreground horses and ponies are tethered for sale. Do the tiers of boxes contain haberdashery items, seeds or corn samples?

SUDBURY, *Thomas Gainsborough's Statue 1934* 86207

The statue was designed by Sir Bertram Mackennal, who also designed the 1908 Olympic medals and the coinage of George V in 1910. The statue is eight-and-a-half feet high on a Portland stone plinth. It was unveiled by Princess Louise, Duchess of Argyll, daughter of Queen Victoria, on 10 June 1913. In the background are Brown & Jay, chemists and oil and colourmen, and the Town Hall.

SUDBURY
St Peter's Church, the Interior c1960
S472040

This shows the church about 12 years before its closure in 1972. In the time of the Rev John Molyneux (1855-79), the church became a bastion of High Church worship, leading to many disputes with the Archdeacon and Bishop. All the pews were sold in the market on 31 March 1859 and replaced with these chairs. The 20-foot-high reredos depicting the crucifixion was designed by George Bodley, who also built the new tower at Long Melford (51170, page 69).

SUDBURY, *Market Hill and St Peter's c1955* S472003

The market is now filled with parked cars, vans, lorries and buses, with at least seven traffic signs in sight. The two hanging signs on the left are for the Black Boy, where King George VI lunched during the Second World War. On the right are the Ideal Fish Restaurant, Lloyds Bank and Joy's fashions. Ahead in Old Market is the roof of Walkers the grocer's, now the Edinburgh Woollen Mill.

▼ **SUDBURY**, *Market Hill and St Peter's c1970* S472035

The shops around the market are becoming dominated by national chains. On the left, for example, are Boots, Foster Brothers and Freeman, Hardy & Willis. On the right the Westminster Bank has replaced Bowles the draper's (see 51156, p.27), Sketchley dry cleaners has replaced the fish shop, and the imposing Lloyds Bank stands next door. Traffic is parked solidly in the centre of the Market Hill; the sides are reserved for buses, and we can make out two single-deckers and a double-decker. Note that the church has now lost its spire; the church was restored in 1969, and the spire was found to be unsafe and was removed.

► **SUDBURY**

The Exchange 1895 35467

This was designed by Henry Kendall in 1841 and opened in 1842. The classical front has four Tuscan columns topped by wheat sheaves instead of urns. The redundant building was converted into a county library in 1968. Next door is Barclays Bank of 1879. Then comes the columned Sudbury Theatre of 1815, which remained the Norwich Fisher Company Theatre until 1848, when it became the Literary and Mechanics' Institute; next door is Potter & Jessop's chemist's shop, later Wardmans. On the corner of Station Road is a three-storey block of Victorian shops. The gable beyond is Thurlows the draper's in Friars Street.

◄ SUDBURY
The Market
1904 51157

We are looking from the west end of Market Hill into Friars Street. Agricultural machinery and fruit and vegetables are set out for sale in front of Frederick Bowles's milliner's and draper's. His shop was to be replaced within a year by the Westminster Bank. On the right is Robert Mattingley's clothing and boot warehouse, and the Anchor, kept by Robert Angier.

► SUDBURY
Friars Street c1955
S472002

On the right is Robert Mattingley's the draper's. This is an 18th-century building with a Venetian window; the upper floor was added in 1892, and has RB in the pediment. Next is the 16th-century Anchor Inn, formerly the White Hart, with Frost's optician's shop in the front. The advertisement for Hills the jeweller's next door is still on the gable. On the left beyond the former theatre is the chemist's shop, latterly Wardmans, which traded here from 1825 to 1975.

SUDBURY
Friars Street Chapel
1900 35477

There had been a Congregational meeting house or chapel on this site since at least 1710. Thomas Gainsborough was baptised in the earlier chapel in 1727. This building was designed in classical style by Frederick Barnes of Ipswich in 1859 at the cost of £1,000; there was seating for 1140 people. The congregation united with Trinity Chapel in School Street in 1956, and the chapel was demolished in 1966.

SUDBURY, *Friars Street Congregational Chapel 1900* 45073

Here we see the interior of the chapel as designed by Frederick Barnes in 1859, with the classical sanctuary filled with the organ. In 1878 Barnes designed the platform, high pulpit, choir stalls and organ case. When the church was demolished, very little was saved. The organ was rebuilt at Ipswich School, and the font became a garden ornament in Great Waldingfield. The minister in 1900 was the Rev Thomas Boyne.

SUDBURY
Friars Street 1895 35468

The imposing 18th-century building on the right with the round-headed doorway has a twin nearly opposite. Next door (beyond the lamp bracket) is where two of Thomas Gainsborough's daughters were born in 1750 and 1751. The awning belongs to Thurlows the draper's, and next door is Woolby's Berlin Wool Warehouse. Opposite, the trees stand front of the Congregational chapel. This side of the chapel is Lucy Berry the confectioner, advertising 'Tea, Coffee and Refreshments'. The notice board in the foreground on the right is advertising the annual fete and firework display.

SUDBURY, *Friars Street 1932* 85141

The railings on the left stand in front of the Congregational chapel of 1859. On the right is an 18th-century house with mansard roof and dormer windows; next door is a brick-built house and shop on the site of the Borough Gaol, demolished c1828. J Rose the tobacconist is in the building with decorative bargeboards. Beyond is Buzzards, the home of Thomas Gainsborough's uncle Thomas; and then F Webb's cycle shop. The spire of St Peter's is just visible in the distance.

▲ SUDBURY
The Grammar School 1904 51163

The Grammar School was founded in 1491 by William Wood of
Sudbury College. These buildings were designed by Robert Page of
London, and opened in 1858 with 26 pupils. The school was vested
in the West Suffolk County Council in 1902 and continued as a
grammar school until 1972, when it became All Saints' Middle
School until 1987. The complex was purchased by Babergh District
Council in 1991 and became William Wood House, sheltered
housing, which was opened by Princess Diana in 1993. On the left is
the spire of Christ Church.

► SUDBURY
Trinity Chapel 1895 35479

This Congregational chapel opened in 1839 as an offshoot from
Friars Street chapel. The name Trinity was chosen to indicate the
group's opposition to Unitarian non-Trinitarian doctrine. The Gothic
west front with a Decorated-style window and the gable tower were
added in 1891 in white brick, almost masking the earlier red-brick
'preaching-box' behind. The congregation united with Friars Street
in 1956 to form Christ Church here, which has been part of the
United Reformed Church since 1975. In 1895 the minister was the
Rev Charles Vine.

SUDBURY
Gainsborough House
1900 45075

In 1722, John Gainsborough purchased two adjacent houses dating from c1480 and 1600; in the following year erected this splendid red-brick Georgian façade with panels below the first floor windows and in the parapet. The plaque, which has since been removed, is inscribed 'In this house was born Thomas Gainsborough, May 1727'. The Gainsborough House Society purchased the house in 1958 and opened it as a museum in 1961.

SUDBURY, *Gainsborough House 1932* 85138

This street, originally called Sepulchre Street, was renamed Gainsborough Street c1910 in honour of the artist. The building was at this time a hotel with tearooms. Adjacent to it are pairs of Victorian houses. Beyond is the Tudor-style Drill Hall of 1881, designed by Arthur Grimwood for D Company 2nd Volunteer Battalion Suffolk Regiment. On the left the tobacconist is advertising Gold Flake. The man and dog have just passed St Gregory's Rectory. Ahead in the distance is the Stone in Stour Street.

► **SUDBURY**
Stour Street 1932
85142

The building on the left is a 16th-century house with a central hall, two cross wings and a later addition at the far end. Most of the 'timbering' shown here was only painted onto the plaster, and has now been covered over. Opposite is the Victorian Stour House, and beyond is Hardwick House, restored in the Arts and Crafts style and used as the Girls' High School until the 1970s.

◄ **SUDBURY**
Salters Hall 1900
45074

The two gables on the left are part of a 15th-century house called The Chantry. The rest of the structure is Salters Hall, the highest quality timber-framed building in Sudbury. The wing nearest to us was built c1450, with a jetty supported by delicate shafts and an oriel window in the gable. The original hall now has an 18th-century mansard roof and a semi-circular window. In 1900 it was the home of Frederick Oates, Esq.

▲ **SUDBURY,** *Mill Common 1932* 85148

From Stour Street we head north along the river. This photograph was taken from the railway line looking east across the Stour. Ahead is the Water and Roller Mill, and to the left is the tower of St Gregory's Church, with the workhouse, or Sudbury Union, now Walnut Tree Hospital, in between. To the right are the houses of Stour and Cross Streets.

◄ **SUDBURY**
The Mill 1895 35484

This is the 18th-century water mill that belonged to Isaac Clover & Sons. The mill is four storeys high, with a central hoist and weather-boarding over the timber frame. The two gabled buildings to the right of the mill had been demolished by 1904. Over to the left is the Sudbury Union Workhouse, about which the Sudbury poet George Fulcher wrote in his 'Village Paupers'.

▶ **SUDBURY**
The Mill 1904 51160

Since 1895 the two buildings to the right of the mill have been replaced by a four-storey brick-built roller mill. The tall silo above the granary fed grain down the chute and over the road into the mill. The chimney, silo and granary hoist have all gone. The mill closed in 1964 and was converted into a hotel in 1972.

◀ **SUDBURY**
Floodgate Pool 1932
85147

The sluice, or floodgate, can be seen on the left; the overflow from it created this pool where the cattle are standing. On the skyline above the sluice are the tower of the Roman Catholic church, buildings along the Croft, the tower of St Gregory's Church, and the workhouse complex.

▶ **SUDBURY**

The River 1893 35486

Just north of Floodgate Pool was the floodgate keeper's cottage, which was demolished in the 1950s. The family out for a stroll have stopped on the path to talk to the gatekeeper. On the right is a jetty in the garden of Croft Lodge. Ahead, the bathing place was to be created the next year behind the line of trees.

◀ **SUDBURY**
The Croft Bridge 1900
45077

This bridge over the Stour leads from The Croft (adjacent to St Gregory's Church on the right) to Fullingpit Meadows, part of Sudbury freemen's land, on the left. Ahead, just left of centre, is the bathing place, and straight ahead are the houses in Melford Road. The bridge has since been replaced, but part of the brick wall to the right remains.

41

▼ **SUDBURY,** *The Bathing Place and the Common 1934* 86208

This was established in 1894, and a bridge was constructed from Little Fullingpit Meadow. Chestnut trees were planted to soften the outline of the semi-circular area, and there were changing cubicles and two springboards. Mixed bathing (even for children) was forbidden. Canvas and metal screens were erected to block the view from the meadows. Children were taught to swim in the shallow area in front of the bar, held up by a harness and rope by the instructor. Then they were allowed to swim beyond the bar and eventually up river. Owing to health problems the complex closed in 1936, to be replaced by Newton Road Baths in 1939.

▶ **SUDBURY**
The Croft and the Roman Catholic Church 1900 45076

On the west side of the green area called the Croft, backing on to the river, are the workhouse and St Gregory's off to the left. Then comes the Presbytery and the red brick Roman Catholic church of St Mary and St John, designed by the Catholic architect Leonard Stokes, which opened in December 1893. The priest in 1900 was Father Augustine Peacock. The large house is the Victorian Croft Lodge with its single-story stable block.

42

◄ SUDBURY
St Gregory's Church c1960
S472006

This is the mother-church of Sudbury, with St Peter's as its chapel-of-ease. The tower is in five stages with a higher stair turret. This end of St Gregory's Street has been radically altered. The buildings on the right were demolished in the late 1960s in a road-widening scheme. The war memorial in North Street was moved to a position outside the church as part of the same development.

► SUDBURY
The Baptist Chapel 1900
35478

There has been a Baptist chapel here since 1834. This chapel was opened in April 1890 at the cost of £2,000 with seating for 600 people. It was designed by William Eade of Ipswich, who used a variety of 13th-century Early English Gothic features, with a rose window in the gable and squat towers. The left door of the house to the left has become a window, the two windows have been shortened, and the Gothic arch of the other door has been removed. Over on the left is the tower of All Saints' Church.

SUDBURY, *St Gregory's, the Interior c1960* S472032

The font cover is one of the finest medieval covers in England, with tabernacle work rising in stages to 12 feet in height. Off to the right is the chapel in which the image of Our Lady of Sudbury stood until 1535. The chancel contains 20 stalls with misericords, which belonged to the college founded by Archbishop Simon of Sudbury in 1375. He was beheaded by the London mob during the Peasant's Revolt of 1381, and his head is preserved in the vestry.

▲ **SUDBURY**
All Saints' Church 1932 85139

The church was mainly rebuilt in the
15th century; for example, money was left for
the north aisle in 1459. Inside is a family tree
of the Eden family of Ballingdon Hall. To the
right is the 18th-century red brick vicarage
with its 19th-century porch. This was the home
of the Rev Samuel Crossman, the hymn writer
who was vicar of All Saints' from 1647 to 1665.
He is best known for his hymns 'My song is
love unknown' and 'Jerusalem on High'.

◀ *detail from* 85139

▶ SUDBURY
The Old Moot Hall 1932 85144

This 15th-century building was either an early Moot (Town) Hall or a Guildhall. The Royal Arms of James I above a ground-floor fireplace may indicate its continuing official use into the 17th century. Externally, the gates at the far end, the right-hand doorway, the ground-floor square bay windows, the lean-to at this end and all the diagonal timbers have been removed since 1932. The carving on the upper floor oriel window, and on another hidden round the corner, is of a high quality.

◀ SUDBURY
Ballingdon Bridge 1900 45079

This was the latest of many wooden bridges to span the River Stour at this point on the main route from Essex (right) into Suffolk. This bridge dates from 1805, and was eventually replaced by one of reinforced concrete in 1911. The medieval hospital of St John stood to the left on the Sudbury side of the bridge.

▲ **SUDBURY,** *Ballingdon Bridge 1934* 86209

This bridge carrying the A131 over the Stour was built of reinforced concrete in 1911. It underwent major repairs in 1983 and was deemed substandard in 1992. After a period of monitoring and a competition inaugurated by the Royal Institute of British Architects in 2000, this bridge was in turn replaced and opened in July 2003. All the buildings on the left, except for the Boathouse Hotel, have been demolished.

◄ **SUDBURY**
Ballingdon Street
1904 51159

This photograph looks from the railway bridge towards the King's Head in Bulmer Road. On the left, the second house with the lower roof has been demolished. On the right the three stylish ladies are approaching the Railway Tavern, now a private house, with its prominent sign over the street. The girl is outside a group of shops with hangings to keep out the heat of the sun. The central building later became Ballingdon Dairy.

FROM SUDBURY TO LAVENHAM

GREAT CORNARD, *The Church 1895* 35488

This view was taken across the River Stour from Middleton in Essex. The tower with its wooden spire containing five bells was restored in 1862. The apparent terracing between the river and the church is actually hedges on either side of the Marks Tey to Sudbury railway line and of the road from Bures to Sudbury running south to north across the photograph. The vicar in 1895 was the Rev William Singleton.

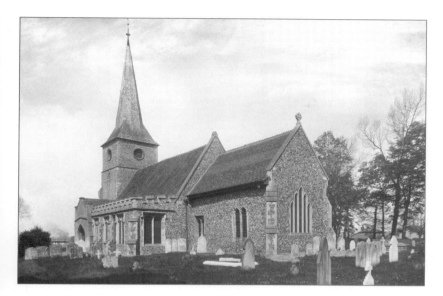

GREAT CORNARD
The Church 1900 45083

The church of St Andrew with its distinctive wooden spire was restored in 1862. The south aisle with its square-headed windows was rebuilt in 1887 by a bequest of William King. The gable cross has gone, and clock faces have been inserted into the tower roundels; otherwise the view is unchanged today.

NEWTON, *The Hotel 1907* 58912

This is the rear view of the Saracen's Head pub; from c1900 to c1930 it was run by Miss Florence Glass, the third generation of her family at the pub since c1850. The pub had its own maltings in the range of buildings alongside. The photograph was taken from the golf course, established in 1907. The A134 Sudbury to Colchester road runs left to right in front of the pub.

NEWTON
The Green 1907 58914

The Newton Green Sudbury Golf Course was established in 1907, and it had its headquarters at the Saracen's Head, visible in the distance. The course '... is over an open common of 52 acres, with nine holes 2,750 yards in length'. The subscriptions in 1910 were £1 9s (£1.45) for gentlemen and 16s (80p) for ladies, with a daily rate of 1s (5p) for visitors. The A134 runs in front of the rows of cottages.

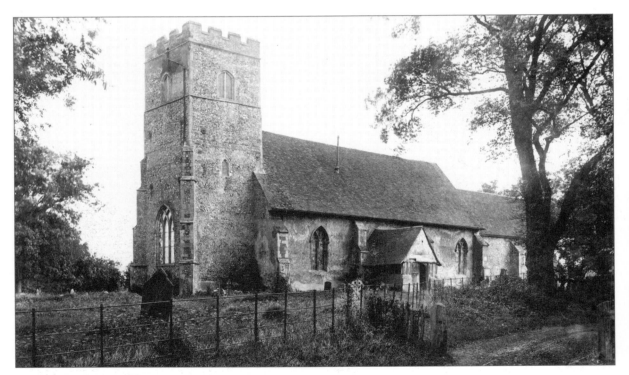

NEWTON, *The Church 1907* 58913a

The nave of All Saints' Church is Norman, with later windows of c1300. Only the chancel is now used for worship; the rest of the building is in the care of the Redundant Churches Fund. The 14th-century wooden porch has been restored and glazed. On the north wall of the nave is a sequence of paintings of the life of the Virgin. The 15th-century pulpit has an inscription asking for prayers for Richard Mondi and Leticie his wife. In the chancel is the canopied effigy of Margaret Boteler (d1410). The rector in 1907 was the Rev Alfred Wren.

GREAT WALDINGFIELD
The Church 1900 45081

The church of St Lawrence was restored in 1876 and the chancel rebuilt in 1869 in the Decorated style by the architect William Butterfield. The 1670s communion rails came from St Michael's, Cornhill, London in the Victorian period. The Rev John Hopkins was rector here from 1561 to 1570; with Thomas Sternhold, he produced the first metrical version of the Psalms in 1562. There is now a lych gate in place of the church gates. The tree to the left is a rare weeping elm, which fell in the storms of 1976. The rector in 1900 was the Rev Charles Stokes.

LITTLE WALDINGFIELD, *The Church 1906* 55559

The church of St Lawrence has twin rood-stair turrets – these are usually found in much larger churches, such as St Mary's, Bury St Edmunds. The south porch dates from 1466. The tower has stone figures at the corners instead of pinnacles. The whole church was restored in 1872. The vicar in 1906 was the Rev John Brown.

51

◢ ACTON
The Church 1906 55558

This 14th-century church contains one of the oldest and finest brasses in England, that of Sir Robert de Bures (d1302). The 18th-century south chapel is 20 feet longer than the chancel, and contains the monument to the Jennens family, including the miser William (d1798). The tower, in ruins here, was rebuilt in 1923, and the bells were re-hung in 1925.

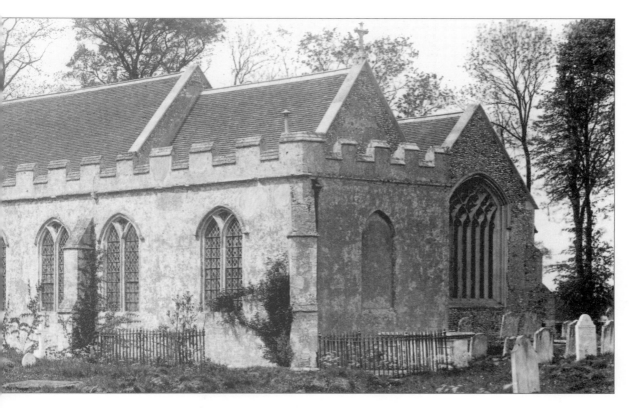

◀ **CHELSWORTH**
*The Bridge and the
Peacock Inn c1965*
C746014

The early 15th-century
Peacock Inn, with its
magnificent cowled central
chimney stack, was named
after a former owner, not the
exotic bird. The River Brett is
spanned by two 18th-century
hump-backed bridges, one of
which is dated 1754. The
house on the right has since
been rebuilt with dormer
windows.

CHELSWORTH
The Peacock Inn
c1960 C746011

The direction sign points to the two bridges over the River Brett. The shop inserted under the jetty (right) closed in 1977. The house beyond has a single-storey shop extension added c1800. The charms of Chelsworth are its timber-framed buildings, which we see here with a variety of external treatments: plaster in the distance, exposed timbers in the centre, and textured plaster panels giving the impression of timbers at the Peacock itself.

CHELSWORTH, *The Village c1960* C746010

The Old Forge dates from c1500; note the blocked mullion window on the side, the double-jettied front and the octagonal 16th-century chimney stacks. In the early 19th century this was the forge and home of Thomas Tampin, the blacksmith. The Village Hall is set back on the left beyond the forge. The River Brett runs parallel to the road over to the right.

MONKS ELEIGH
The Swingleton
c1965 M270008

This small hamlet to the south of Monks Eleigh, at the foot of Back Lane, may derive its name from the making of swingles, the hinged business-end of a flail. The nearest house is the Old Bakery, followed by Church's, a medieval hall house. At the end, to the right, is the roof of the 16th-century Hobarts.

MONKS ELEIGH, *The Street c1955* M270003

The thatched 15th-century Swan Inn, owned by Ind Coope, closed in 1983 and reopened as a free house in 1984. Following the closure of the post office and stores in March 2003, a community shop and post office opened in the barn of the Swan in December 2003. The single-decker bus is approaching another now closed shop selling Walls ice cream.

MONKS ELEIGH
The Village c1955
M270001

The monks referred to in the village's name are the monks of Canterbury, who were lords of the manor and patrons of the living. The pump in the foreground was made by Ransomes & Sims of Ipswich; it was presented to the village in 1854 by William Makin of Hall Farm, which can be seen to the right of the church. The white Gothic archway on the left was the entrance to the school, built in the grounds of the former parish workhouse.

► **MONKS ELEIGH**
The Village c1955
M270024

The tapering village green leads up to St Peter's Church. The 15th-century tower with flushwork battlements and pinnacles had a short spire until 1845. The clock dates from 1841, and the bell hangs above the tall stair turret. The 17th-century thatched barn on the right is part of the Monks Eleigh Hall Farm. Christopher Wordsworth, younger brother of the poet, was rector here from 1811 to 1816.

◄ **BRENT ELEIGH**
Street Farm c1960
B615007

The River Brett curves around the farmhouse, now at the blocked end of the village street nearest to Monks Eleigh. The building dates from c1480, although brick and plaster cover the timber frame. Its present appearance dates from 1880, when it was part of the estate owned by Walter Brown of Brent Eleigh Hall.

▲ **BRENT ELEIGH,** *The Street c1960* B615006

The post office, now Swan Cottage, displayed advertisements for Walls ice cream and Bird's Eye frozen foods. The wooden cycle stand is positioned in front of the bay window with its tempting display. The post office closed c1972. The thatched extension at this end of the medieval High Bank has since been demolished. The street is now a cul-de-sac, following the opening of the by-pass in the 1980s.

◀ **BRENT ELEIGH**
The Street c1960
B615005

On the left, the new chalet bungalow is for sale. The weatherboarded former water mill, trading as Brent Eleigh Tools (centre left), was converted into a dwelling c1990; the mill machinery and stones were preserved in the conversion. The red brick almshouses on the right, founded by Edward Coleman in 1731, were modernised in 1966. Beyond is High Bank, a medieval hall house.

LAVENHAM

LAVENHAM, *Water Street c1955* L21012

The house on the right was known as Garrards until 1926, when it was partly demolished, but owing to local protest it was restored again, and is now called de Vere House. The doorway has the de Vere star and boar with flanking figures, all of which were there in 1926. Beyond are groups of once jettied cottages. The street takes its name from the stream which rises at Lavenham Hall and once flowed down the street.

▼ **LAVENHAM,** *Lady Street c1955* L21013

This street takes its name from the Guildhall of Our Lady, later called the Wool Hall, which now forms part of the Swan Hotel on the left. Parts of the building were dismantled in 1911, but were restored in 1913 by Princess Louise, Duchess of Argyll, who opened it as a Railway Workers Home. On the right are Tudor Shops, a high quality Tudor range, with arched shop windows on the ground floor, restored between 1978 and 1981.

► **LAVENHAM**
Lady Street c1960
L21008

In the centre of the picture, in Water Street, is Priory Farm, which once belonged to Earls Colne Priory in Essex. It was later owned by the Rev Henry Copinger, rector of Lavenham from 1578 to 1622, whose monument in the chancel was restored in 2004. The Wool Hall was incorporated into the Swan Hotel (right) between 1963 and 1965; Tudor Shops are on the left.

◄**LAVENHAM**
The Guildhall
1904 51180

This was built c1529 for Corpus Christi guild, and it was used until guilds were abolished in 1547. The guild was a combination of a club and an insurance policy, in as much as the deceased members would be prayed for to shorten their time in purgatory. The timber work and carving is of outstanding quality; there is a carved porch, a bressummer beam, corner posts, original windows and an oriel window towards Lady Street. The building had a variety of later uses, including a jail, a workhouse and an almshouse.

LAVENHAM
The Guildhall c1955
L21007

In 1887 the Guildhall and the adjoining properties were purchased and restored by Sir Cuthbert Quilter of Bawdsey Manor, who was also MP for the Sudbury Division. In 1944 the Lavenham Preservation Committee was formed to preserve Lavenham's buildings, especially the Guildhall. In 1951 the Quilter family and the Committee vested the property in the National Trust, who maintain it today.

LAVENHAM
Market Place c1955 L21006

The market cross was given by William Jacob, a clothier, in 1500; it is a copy of the cross at Cambridge, an indication of how Lavenham saw itself at the time. To the left is the Great House, a restaurant since 1983, and the Little Hall of 1425-50, now the home of the Suffolk Preservation Society, the successor to the Lavenham Preservation Committee. Ahead is the medieval Market Toll House, restored in 1978, when the jetty was reinstated.

LAVENHAM, *The Church 1895* 35497

This is one of the best-known churches in England. It was rebuilt, except for the 14th-century chancel, between c1485 and 1525. The money was provided by the de Veres, Earls of Oxford and lords of the manor, the Spring family, wealthy clothiers, and many others connected with the woollen cloth trade. The exterior bears shields and heraldic devices of the de Vere and Spring families to show which parts they built. Like Long Melford, part of the church extends to the east of the chancel, in this case a vestry.

LAVENHAM, *The Church Porch c1955* L21002

Most of the nave and aisles and the porch were paid for by John de Vere, 13th Earl of Oxford, of Castle Hedingham and Lavenham. The porch is decorated with the de Vere stars, coats of arms and two boars, often mistaken for sheep, a play on words, as 'verres' is Latin for a boar pig. During a restoration in 1965, statues of St Peter and St Paul by Eric Winters were placed in the central niche, a gift of the Friends of Lavenham Church.

LONG
MELFORD

LONG MELFORD, *Kentwell Hall 1895* 35495

Kentwell is at the north end of the village, approached by a mile-long avenue of lime trees planted in 1678. The earlier manor house was the home of John Clopton, who coordinated the rebuilding of the church in the late 15th century. This building, begun in the 1540s, was described as 'new' in 1563, and was extended in the 1590s. In 1895 the house was owned by Edward Starkie-Bence, but leased to Henry Norton.

► **LONG MELFORD**
The Church 1895
35493

The church was almost entirely rebuilt between the 1460s and 1490s. The exterior has lengthy inscriptions and dates recording those who gave money to the various parts of the building. An almost unique feature is the Lady Chapel, positioned east of the chancel and built by John Clopton in 1496. Inside it is a church in miniature, with aisles on all four sides for processions around the shrine of Our Lady of Melford, which was removed in 1547.

► *(far right) detail from* 35493

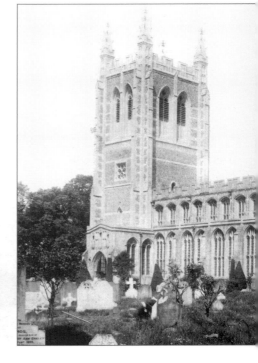

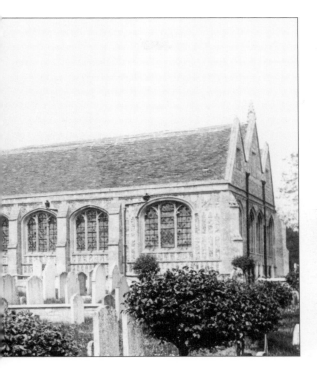

◄ **LONG MELFORD**
The Church 1904
51170

The magnificence of the church was rather spoilt by the 18th-century red brick tower with classical blank arches and windows (see photograph 35493), built after much of the medieval tower fell in 1700. This was replaced to celebrate the Diamond Jubilee of Queen Victoria in 1887. The architect was George Bodley; he designed a Gothic tower so much in sympathy with the building that many visitors are unaware that it was only completed in 1903.

◄ *(far left) detail from*
51170

▶ **LONG MELFORD**
The Green and Melford Hall c1955 L101004

This is taken from the north end of the Green, looking south towards Hall Street, showing the wide expanse of the Green, where fairs are still held. On the left is the 19th-century red brick Tudor-style gatehouse to Melford Hall. Behind are the pinnacles of the octagonal Tudor summerhouse in the corner of the Hall gardens. The group of trees was felled in 1979 as a result of Dutch elm disease.

◄ LONG MELFORD
Melford Hall 1895 35492

This early Elizabethan mansion was built on the site of the former house of the abbot of Bury St Edmunds by Sir William Cordell, Master of the Rolls, who founded the hospital on the Green. The original plan was an open courtyard with rooms on all four sides. The wing nearest to us was removed in the early 17th century to obtain a view over the park. Queen Elizabeth visited in 1578, and the Prince and Princess of Wales in 1864. The owner and lord of the manor in 1893 was the Rev Sir William Hyde. The house now belongs to the National Trust, although the Hyde-Parker family continue to live there.

◄ *(far left) detail from* 35492

▼ **LONG MELFORD,** *The Church, the Interior 1900* 35494

The three piers of the nave nearest to us were retained from the earlier 14th-century church when the great rebuilding took place in the late 15th century. This style of building, with no chancel arch and a continuous roof, was common in large churches of this period. The stone reredos dates from 1879; its design is based on the description of the pre-Reformation reredos by Roger Martin of Melford Place, whose brass is in the south chapel. The tomb of Sir William Cordell (d1581) is on the right side of the sanctuary.

► **LONG MELFORD**
The Bull Hotel
c1955 L101002

The building dates from c1450 and has been an inn since at least 1532. The Victorian brick façade was removed in 1935 to reveal the timber framing. The doorposts have initials of the Drew family and the date 1649. In the 1960s an extension incorporating the chimney stack was built to the right. The children (left) are in Bull Lane, leading to Acton.

◄LONG MELFORD
Little St Mary's
c1955 L101010

We have now nearly reached the southern end of the street, and have turned round to head back to the church. The building on the right is a substantial medieval house with later additions. Gardiner's Garage next door, now a dress shop, was originally a maltings. Further up, the tall house with a Georgian façade was the doctor's surgery for much of the 19th and 20th centuries. The maltings beyond is one of several antique warehouses in the village. Much of the BBC 'Lovejoy' series was filmed in the village.

LONG MELFORD
Hall Street c1955
L101008

This view shows the great width of the street running north to the Green and the church. On the left is the 16th-century Old House Country Club, now Chimney's Restaurant; in the 1830s John Churchyard lived here - he started the horse-hair weaving industry in Melford. Next is the 1830s brick Foundry House, where Ward & Silver's iron foundry was established in the 1840s. Many of their cast-iron grave markers can be seen in the churchyard.

► **LONG MELFORD**
Hall Street c1955
L101011

This photograph shows
Little Green with Hall Water
Mill on the left side. The
name Melford probably
derived from 'mill on the
ford'. The famous Bull Hotel
with its gables and wide
chimney stack is on the
right, adjacent to Bull Lane.
The group of cottages to
the right was demolished
in the 1960s to make way
for an extension to the hotel.

◄ LONG MELFORD
The Green 1906
55557

In the distance is the church, partly obscured by the Hospital of the Holy Trinity founded in 1573 by Sir William Cordell of Long Melford Hall. Along the western edge of the Green, medieval and Tudor houses have either been subdivided into workers' cottages, or given Georgian façades. The children on the Green have just come out of the National School, off to the left. John Whitehead was the schoolmaster, Elizabeth Robertson the girls' mistress and Miss McBeath the infants' mistress.

LONG MELFORD
The Green and the Black Lion Hotel c1955 L101005

This is the north end of Melford Green with the road to Stanstead to the left. The Black Lion was rebuilt in c1840, but stands on the site of an earlier inn of the same name, which can be traced back to c1660. On the left is Ye Olde Top Shoppe, 'high class grocery and provisions', which closed in the 1970s and is now a house. Ahead, Church Walk leads up to the hospital, rebuilt in 1847, the church and the rectory.

FROM LONG MELFORD TO SUDBURY

STANSTEAD
The Church c1965 S182020

The church is mainly 15th-century, with the exception of the 14th-century tower with its chequerboard flushwork on the parapet. The south porch has finials with dragons instead of pinnacles. Inside there is a mosaic and marble monument to the Rev Samuel Sheen (d1867) and a window to his son Samuel (d1907), who was also rector here.

GLEMSFORD
The Church 1904
51178

The south chapel, hidden behind the church, dates from 1497. The external flushwork decoration on the chapel, porch and south aisle is almost identical to that on the Lady Chapel at Long Melford. They are both the work of the master mason John of Melford (d1509). Following the fall of Thurston church tower in March 1860, the tower here was examined and found to be unstable; rebuilding began in July 1860. Is the donkey just passing by, or waiting for Palm Sunday?

GLEMSFORD, *Tye Green c1960* G235005

The tall building behind the hip-roofed thatched cottage is a water tower, which has since been demolished. The general stores and fish and chip shop were owned by D A Chatters. A nearby road is named after the Rev Harpur, vicar here from 1937 to 1950, who lived in the former vicarage on the left. In Suffolk, Tye is the local name for a small green.

PENTLOW
The Church of St George and St Gregory 1904 51176

The nave and apsidal chancel are Norman. The round tower was added to the nave in the 12th century, and the original highly carved Norman west door of the nave now leads into the tower. The square font is also Norman, with a 15th-century cover with door opening on the side. The church had been recently restored in 1887 by William Fawcett of Cambridge. The rector in 1904 was the Rev Felix Bull.

BULMER, *The Church 1906* 55557a

The chancel of St Andrew's was restored in 1883, when all the stonework was renewed, but retaining the 14th-century detail of the windows. The nave, and the north aisle with its cat-slide roof, were restored in 1891, but are originally of the 15th century. The vicar in 1906 was the Rev Arthur Pannell. Inside is a monument to Robert and Frances Andrews of Auberies, who in 1749 were the subject of one of Gainsborough's most famous paintings.

FOXEARTH, *The Church of St Peter and St Paul 1904* 51177

The patron and rector from 1845 to 1892 was the Rev John Foster, who restored the church on High Church Anglo-Catholic principles. The tower with its tall lancet windows divided by louvres and its broach spire, designed by Henry Woodyear in 1862, blew down in 1947. Internally, all the pre-Reformation church furnishings were replaced by exact Victorian copies, including altar, reredos, rood-screen, wall paintings and stained glass. The rector in 1904 was the Rev William Pressey.

▲ MIDDLETON
The Arch 1906 55552

Known as the Prince of Wales Arch, this was erected by the Rev Oliver Raymond (d1889), the third of six Raymonds who were rectors here. He rebuilt the house, and diverted local roads and created a park with avenues of trees on his glebe land. The arch commemorates the birth of the Prince of Wales, later King Edward VII, in 1841. The re-used stones feature the de Vere star, and came from Earl's Colne Priory.

◄ MIDDLETON
The Church 1895 35489

The church has a Norman nave and chancel, with Norman mouldings to the south door and chancel arch. The porch is Tudor. The single bell is housed in an 18th-century bellcote with an ornate Gothic spire - this has since been removed down to the tops of the windows. The rector in 1895 was the Rev Oliver Edward Raymond.

► **SUDBURY**
Ladies Bridge 1923
73607

Before the creation of
Ladies Island, as a result
of straightening the
River Stour in the 1950s,
Ladies Bridge carried the
footpath from Cornard Road
over the river. To the right
was a canal and railway
siding, where barges were
loaded with lime and
bricks for the local and
London markets.

◄ **SUDBURY**
Ballingdon Hall 1904 51162

The house was built for Sir Thomas Eden in c1593, of which only this range remains. In 1972 the 170-ton building was moved a quarter of a mile to a position 60 feet higher than the original site over a period of 52 days. The owners, Angela and John Hodge, wanted more privacy as housing developments drew nearer. They were able to occupy the house again in 1975.

LAVENHAM, *From the air 1972* AFA228526

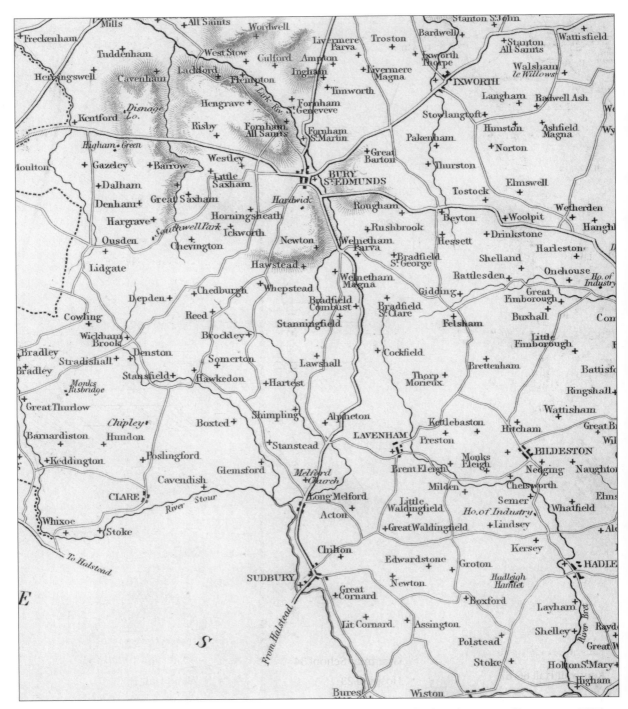

SUFFOLK COUNTY MAP, *showing Sudbury, Lavenham and Long Melford and surrounding areas c1850*

INDEX

NAMES OF PRE-PUBLICATION BUYERS

The following people have kindly supported this book by subscribing to copies before publication.

The Ablitt Family

P E T Allen, Long Melford

The Alston & Pilgrim Families

Mr Roy Alston, Red House, Long Melford

Patrick & Pamela Arbon, Sudbury

Tom & May Bailey, Sudbury

G R & J A Baldwin

In memory of Dorothy E Bareham, Sudbury

Ron Bennett, In memory of L & V Bennett

Norman & Thelma Best, Sudbury, with love

Mrs J Black, Sudbury

In memory of Desmond Boggis of Sudbury

Valentine Joy Boyden, Sudbury, Suffolk

Happy Anniversary, Brenda & Roy

The Bridges Family, Little Waldingfield

Susan M Brotherwood, Sudbury

Mrs G I Bugg

Mr M R & Mrs S A Bugg

D G Butcher, Sudbury Police Supt. 1945-58

K M Butcher, Walnut Tree Hospital 1961-89

In memory of Tom Cameron

Edward Carter

The Carter Family, Chapel Green, Melford

Remembering The Cawstons

Adrian Chapman & Gary England, Sudbury

Mr Donald Chatters

Rob, Mel, Aaron & Taryn Chinnery, Sudbury

In memory of Alfred & Nell Clark, Sudbury

Mr & Mrs E Clarke, Long Melford

In memory of John Cole, loved by all, Mum

Leonard Cole, Acton

Gerald & Philippa Cook, Long Melford

Babs & Mick Cornish, Great Cornard

L J Crumpton-Taylor, Gestingthorpe, Essex

To Dad from Roger and Sharon

Mr & Mrs R Davidson, Sudbury

The De'ath Family, Sudbury

Mr & Mrs Michael Dixon, Little Yeldham

Mr T A & Mrs M A Drake, Great Cornard

Betty Draper (nee Nicholls)

To the Family of Bryan M R Duce

John, Mary, Catherine & Jonathan Dunlea

The Dyer Family, Sudbury

Steve & Marianne Edwards, Sudbury

Roger Eve on his 60th Birthday

David Everitt, Sudbury

In memory of F Paul Fayers, to his sons

In memory of Joan Finch, the Benham Family, Long Melford

The Garrard Family, Lavenham

Joe Goble QGM & Jan Goble, Sudbury

Mr R G & Mrs D Grantham, Great Cornard

In memory of Terence W Hamblett, Sudbury

To a special person, Anne Hately

Peter & Rosemary Haynes, Glemsford

The Hearnden Family, Milden

Nick Herbert on your 40th Birthday

The Hockley Family, Sudbury

Gerald & Sue Horsley, Great Cornard

Ken Horsley, Sudbury

In memory of Mr & Mrs R A Houlden, Sudbury

Mr D M & Mrs D J Howard, Chilton

Christine & Dennis Ingram of Lavenham

To Peter Jackson from Alice & Harriet

To our friends Jan & Greg, Victoria, Australia

To Grandad John on his birthday

The Jolly & Elmer Families, Sudbury

In Memory of Beatrice Jones, Sudbury

Mr H & Mrs P Jones

Phyllis Kiddy, Sudbury

To Jean King, on her birthday, love Bev

Margaret & John King, Glemsford

Landers Bookshop of Long Melford

In memory of Margaret M Lawrence

In memory of John F K Leggett of Sudbury

Katherine Long, Glemsford

Theresa Long, Glemsford

Jane Lowe, Sudbury

The Ludlow Family of Great Cornard

Glen & Vashti Reid Ludlow & Family

Simon & Karen Ludlow of Great Cornard

Mr & Mrs C J Lushey, Long Melford

James P McGregor, born in Glemsford 16/01/02

In memory of Jack Medcalf, Sudbury

In memory of Albert & Chelia Miller

Mr D A Mills

Mrs Napier

In memory of the Nicholls Family, Sudbury

I G Norman & M R Norman, Sudbury

The Northcott Family, Great Cornard

John & Vivian Outen, Weavers Lane, Sudbury

M J H Pearson

Lesley & Tony Platt, Little Cornard

The Powell Family, Long Melford

Mrs J Purkiss & Mrs M Drury

Ray Rainbird, Acton

Mr R H & Mrs I J Rawden, Long Melford

The Reading Family, Long Melford

Brian H Reeman & the Reeman Family, Alpheton

G, C & L Riches, Chilton, Sudbury

For John Rimmer, Artist and Philosopher

To Roger on his birthday love Ula 2005

Kenneth J Rooney, Sudbury

The Roper Family, Long Melford

Alan William Sandford 31-01-42

Brian Semark, Carol Semark

Thomas A Sharkey, Sudbury

June D Sharp, Sudbury

To a wonderful Mum, Diane Sharpe

D J Slater

The Angelo Smith Family, Sudbury

Wendy Steele, Sudbury

Ronald Norman Street, Glemsford

Suffolk Free Press

John Sullivan, Brent Eleigh, 2005

In memory of Mr & Mrs D Suttle, Melford

Gloria Anne Tatum, Sudbury

Colin Taylor, Great Cornard

John & Gillian Taylor

The late Arthur & Doris Tooley, Cornard

Mrs D Walker, Long Melford

James Walker, Long Melford

Susan Walker, Sudbury

The Wallace Family, Great Cornard

Mr C R T & Mrs N A Wallace, Lavenham

Tracey A Wallace, Long Melford

Mr P A & Mrs J A Warner & boys, Sudbury

Brian Watts & Son Upholstery, Long Melford

Elizabeth Wigmore, Gt Walingfield

Neil & Maria Williams, January 2005

Roger & Elaine Williams, Little Waldingfield

Val & Fred Witt, Sudbury

The Wood Family, Newton Green

Mr A & Mrs C Woodcock, Long Melford

Graham & Rose Woodward, Sudbury

Mr D C Wright, Sudbury

R & E Wright, 'For our Memories', Mum & Dad

Nicholas Younger of Sudbury

FRITH PRODUCTS & SERVICES

Francis Frith would doubtless be pleased to know that the pioneering publishing venture he started in 1860 still continues today. Over a hundred and forty years later, The Francis Frith Collection continues in the same innovative tradition and is now one of the foremost publishers of vintage photographs in the world. Some of the current activities include:

Interior Decoration

Today Frith's photographs can be seen framed and as giant wall murals in thousands of pubs, restaurants, hotels, banks, retail stores and other public buildings throughout the country. In every case they enhance the unique local atmosphere of the places they depict and provide reminders of gentler days in an increasingly busy and frenetic world.

Product Promotions

Frith products are used by many major companies to promote the sales of their own products or to reinforce their own history and heritage. Frith promotions have been used by Hovis bread, Courage beers, Scots Porage Oats, Colman's mustard, Cadbury's foods, Mellow Birds coffee, Dunhill pipe tobacco, Guinness, and Bulmer's Cider.

Genealogy and Family History

As the interest in family history and roots grows world-wide, more and more people are turning to Frith's photographs of Great Britain for images of the towns, villages and streets where their ancestors lived; and, of course, photographs of the churches and chapels where their ancestors were christened, married and buried are an essential part of every genealogy tree and family album.

Frith Products

All Frith photographs are available Framed or just as Mounted Prints and Posters (size 23 x 16 inches). These may be ordered from the address below. From time to time other products - Address Books, Maps, etc - are available.

The Internet

Already fifty thousand Frith photographs can be viewed and purchased on the internet through the Frith websites and a myriad of partner sites.

For more detailed information on Frith companies and products, look at these sites:

www.francisfrith.co.uk
www.francisfrith.com
(for North American visitors)

See the complete list of Frith Books at:

www.francisfrith.co.uk

This web site is regularly updated with the latest list of publications from the Frith Book Company. If you wish to buy books relating to another part of the country that your local bookshop does not stock, you may purchase on-line.

For further information, trade, or author enquiries please contact us at the address below:
The Francis Frith Collection, Frith's Barn, Teffont, Salisbury, Wiltshire, England SP3 5QP.
Tel: +44 (0)1722 716 376 Fax: +44 (0)1722 716 881   Email: sales@francisfrith.co.uk

See Frith books on the internet at www.francisfrith.co.uk

FREE PRINT OF YOUR CHOICE

Mounted Print
Overall size 14 x 11 inches (355 x 280mm)

Choose any Frith photograph in this book.
Simply complete the Voucher opposite and
return it with your remittance for £2.25 (to cover
postage and handling) and we will print the
photograph of your choice in SEPIA (size 11 x 8
inches) and supply it in a cream mount with a
burgundy rule line (overall size 14 x 11 inches).
**Please note: photographs with a reference
number starting with a "Z" are not Frith
photographs and cannot be supplied under
this offer.**
Offer valid for delivery to one UK address only.

PLUS: **Order additional Mounted Prints
at HALF PRICE - £7.49 each** (normally £14.99)
If you would like to order more Frith prints from
this book, possibly as gifts for friends and family,
you can buy them at half price (with no
additional postage and handling costs).

PLUS: **Have your Mounted Prints framed**
For an extra £14.95 per print you can have your
mounted print(s) framed in an elegant polished
wood and gilt moulding, overall size 16 x
13 inches (no additional postage and handling
required).

IMPORTANT!

**These special prices are only available if you use
this form to order . You must use the ORIGINAL
VOUCHER on this page (no copies permitted). We
can only despatch to one UK address. This offer
cannot be combined with any other offer.**

Send completed Voucher form to:
**The Francis Frith Collection, Frith's Barn,
Teffont, Salisbury, Wiltshire SP3 5QP**

CHOOSE A PHOTOGRAPH FROM THIS BOOK

Voucher for **FREE** and *Reduced Price Frith Prints*

*Please do not photocopy this voucher. Only the original is valid,
so please fill it in, cut it out and return it to us with your order.*

Picture ref no	Page no	Qty	Mounted @ £7.49	Framed + £14.95	Total Cost £
		1	Free of charge*	£	£
			£7.49	£	£
			£7.49	£	£
			£7.49	£	£
			£7.49	£	£
			£7.49	£	£

*Please allow 28 days
for delivery.
Offer available to one
UK address only*

* Post & handling	£2.25
Total Order Cost	£

Title of this book . . . .
I enclose a cheque/postal order for £ . . . .
made payable to 'The Francis Frith Collection'

OR please debit my Mastercard / Visa / Maestro / Amex
card, details below

Card Number

Issue No (Maestro only)   Valid from (Maestro)

Expires   Signature

Name Mr/Mrs/Ms . . . .
Address . . . .
. . . .
. . . .
. . . . Postcode . . . .
Daytime Tel No . . . .
Email . . . .

ISBN: 1-85937-850-1   Valid to 31/12/07

Would you like to find out more about Francis Frith?

We have recently recruited some entertaining speakers who are happy to visit local groups, clubs and societies to give an illustrated talk documenting Frith's travels and photographs. If you are a member of such a group and are interested in hosting a presentation, we would love to hear from you.

Our speakers bring with them a small selection of our local town and county books, together with sample prints. They are happy to take orders. A small proportion of the order value is donated to the group who have hosted the presentation. The talks are therefore an excellent way of fundraising for small groups and societies.

Can you help us with information about any of the Frith photographs in this book?

We are gradually compiling an historical record for each of the photographs in the Frith archive. It is always fascinating to find out the names of the people shown in the pictures, as well as insights into the shops, buildings and other features depicted.

If you recognize anyone in the photographs in this book, or if you have information not already included in the author's caption, do let us know. We would love to hear from you, and will try to publish it in future books or articles.

Our production team

Frith books are produced by a small dedicated team at offices in the converted Grade II listed 18th-century barn at Teffont near Salisbury, illustrated above. Most have worked with the Frith Collection for many years. All have in common one quality: they have a passion for the Frith Collection. The team is constantly expanding, but currently includes:

Paul Baron, Phillip Brennan, Jason Buck, John Buck, Ruth Butler, Heather Crisp, David Davies, Louis du Mont, Isobel Hall, Lucy Hart, Julian Hight, Peter Horne, James Kinnear, Karen Kinnear, Tina Leary, Stuart Login, David Marsh, Lesley-Ann Millard, Sue Molloy, Glenda Morgan, Wayne Morgan, Sarah Roberts, Kate Rotondetto, Dean Scource, Eliza Sackett, Terence Sackett, Sandra Sampson, Adrian Sanders, Sandra Sanger, Julia Skinner, Miles Smith, Lewis Taylor, Shelley Tolcher, Lorraine Tuck, David Turner, Amanita Wainwright and Ricky Williams.